28

Machines Inside Machines

Using Pulleys and Gears

Wendy Sadler

Raintree

Chicago, Illinois

For information address the publisher:
Raintree, 100 N. LaSalle, Suite 1200, Chicago, IL 60602

Printed and bound in China by South China Printing Company

09 08 07 06 05
10 9 8 7 6 5 4 3 2 1

Library of Congress Cataloging-in-Publication Data:
Cataloging-in-Publication Data is on file at the Library of Congress.

ISBN 1-4109-1445-3 (lib. binding), 1-4109-1452-6 (Pbk.)

Acknowledgments
The publishers would like to thank the following for permission to reproduce photographs:
Alamy Images (Leslie Garland Picture Library) p. **11**; Alamy Images (Leslie Garland Picture Library) pp. **13, 26**; Alamy Images (SCPhotos) pp. **6, 14**; Corbis (Mark Hanauer) p. **5**; Corbis (Sygma/Sandy Huffaker JR) p. **4**; Corbis (Craig Aurness) p. **24**; Corbis (John & Lisa Merrill) p. **19**; Corbis (Kevin Fleming) p. **9**; Corbis (Owen Franken) p. **7**; Corbis (Ron Watts) p. **12**; Corbis (Tim de Waele) p. **21**; DK Images p. **27**; Harcourt Education Ltd (Trevor Clifford) pp. **16, 22**; Harcourt Education Ltd (Tudor Photography) pp. **18, 20, 23, 25**; Peter Willis p. **29**; Powerstock (age fotostock) p. **15**.

Cover photograph of cogs reproduced with permission of Getty Images (Taxi)

Every effort has been made to contact copyright holders of any material reproduced in this book. Any omissions will be rectified in subsequent printings if notice is given to the publishers.

Disclaimer:
All the Internet addresses (URLs) given in this book were valid at the time of going to press. However, due to the dynamic nature of the Internet, some addresses may have changed, or sites may have changed or ceased to exist since publication. While the author and Publishers regret any inconvenience this may cause readers, no responsibility for any such changes can be accepted by either the author or the Publishers.

Contents

Any words appearing in the text in bold, **like this,** are explained in the glossary.

Machines with Pulleys or Gears

Pulleys are **simple machines.** A simple machine is something that helps us to do a job. Pulleys are made up of parts that include a wheel, an **axle,** and some rope. They are usually used to help people lift things up. You can find pulleys all around you.

Pulleys are being used on this boat to lower a whale back into the sea.

Gears are simple machines made up of a set of wheels with "teeth" around the edges. These wheels with teeth are called **cogs.** The cogs are linked together.

Gears are useful for changing the speed or direction of something that turns or spins. There are gears on bicycles and inside car **engines.** Different types of gear can make things move in different ways.

Gears on a bicycle help us to ride up steep hills.

Fixed Pulleys

If you have curtains in your house, they might use a pulley. When you want to open the curtains and see out of the window, you pull down on the string. The pulley opens the curtains. This is a **fixed pulley.**

Have you used a pulley like this before?

A fixed pulley has a wheel that does not move from its position. It only turns around and around.

Flagpoles have fixed pulleys. The flag starts off at the bottom of the pole. When you pull down on the rope, the other end moves up. The flag is attached to this end, so it also moves up the pole.

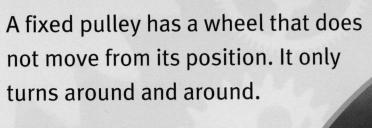

A fixed pulley changes the direction of the **force** you put in, but not the amount of force you need to do the job.

Moving Pulleys

There are two types of pulley: a **fixed pulley** and a **movable pulley.** A movable pulley uses a wheel that is not fixed in one place, so it can move along the rope. The moving part of the pulley is usually joined to the object you want to lift. The other end of the rope is fixed to something solid above the object you want to lift.

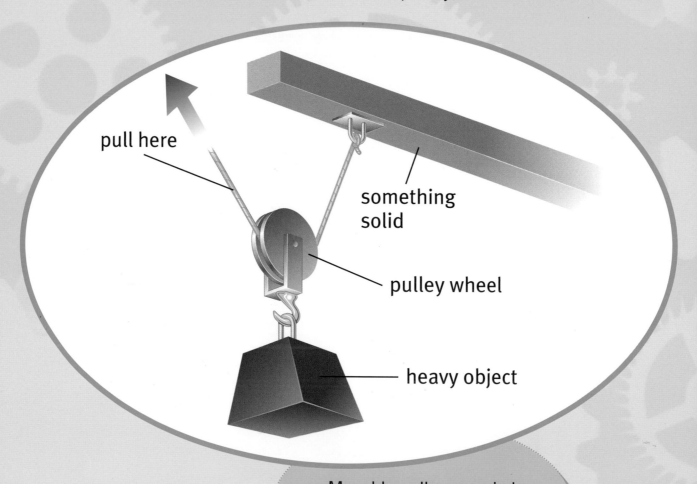

pull here

something solid

pulley wheel

heavy object

Movable pulleys can help you lift heavy objects you would not be able to lift on your own.

With a single movable pulley, you have to use your **effort force** and pull in the same direction as the object you want to lift. You need to pull the rope over a longer distance, but you need less effort force to lift the weight.

Climbers sometimes use movable pulleys to rescue other climbers who have fallen. A movable pulley is attached to a rope on a climber's belt. The other end is attached to another climber who also has a pulley on his or her belt. If one climber falls, the other can use the movable pulley to help pull him or her back to safety.

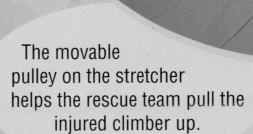
The movable pulley on the stretcher helps the rescue team pull the injured climber up.

Combined Pulleys

A **combined pulley** has at least two wheels that turn as you pull on a rope. This is the most useful way to use pulleys.

Combined pulleys usually have one **fixed pulley** at the top, which is joined to something solid. There is also usually one **movable pulley,** which is joined onto the object that you are trying to lift. The fixed pulley changes the direction of the **force** you put in. The movable pulley increases your force so that you can lift heavy weights.

Combined pulleys are very useful machines!

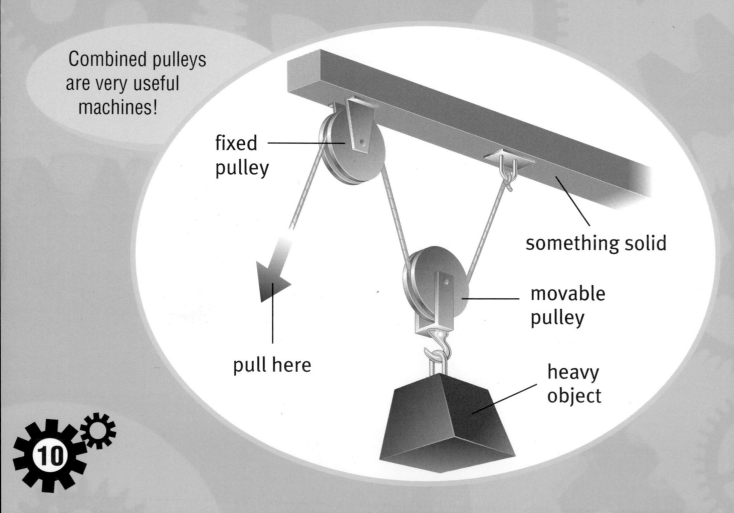

fixed pulley

something solid

movable pulley

pull here

heavy object

A pulley gives you something called a **mechanical advantage.** Mechanical advantage happens when you get more force out of a machine than you put into it. This means it reduces the **effort force** you need to lift something.

A combined pulley with two wheels needs half the effort force that you would need to lift something without a pulley. This means you can lift twice as much as your effort force when you use a pulley.

Pulleys are helping this man lift his boat out of the water.

How Much Do Pulleys Help Us?

People can use pulleys to help them clean very tall buildings. They sit on seats with ropes attached to them and to the top of the building. The ropes go around a **combined pulley.** Electric **motors** help pull the ropes that move the seats up and down. By using pulleys, the motor does not have to pull all the weight of each seat. It can pull with much less **force,** but it has to pull the ropes a long distance.

This man is using a pulley to help him clean the windows of a very tall building.

Cranes

Cranes can lift very heavy objects such as cars, trucks, and big bricks for building houses. They use lots of pulleys to help reduce the amount of force needed.

A crane has lots of combined pulleys working together. Motors wind up their rope. Because the weights they lift are very heavy, the motors have to wind the rope a long way.

Cranes use pulleys to help lift very heavy weights such as these buildings blocks.

What would happen without . . . ?

We need cranes to help us build tall buildings. Without cranes, all our buildings would probably be less than four stories high.

People and Pulleys

At the gym, some people use machines with pulleys to lift weights. The machines exercise different parts of the body. Pulleys are used to change the direction of **force** that you need to lift the weights. For example, you might push down to lift a weight up. This means that they usually use a **fixed pulley.**

This machine has a handle that people pull down on to exercise.

In some countries, people have to get their water from a well. The water in the well is very deep under the ground. It would be hard to reach without a rope. A bucket of water is heavy to lift, so a fixed pulley at the top of the well makes it easier. People need less force to lift the water, and they can use the weight of their bodies to help them pull.

A pulley on a well helps to lift heavy buckets of water out of the ground.

What Is a Gear?

A gear is made up of two or more **cogs.** A cog is a wheel that has "teeth" around the edge. The teeth in the cogs fit together. When the first cog turns, the teeth push against the teeth in the second cog. This makes the second cog turn in the opposite direction. If you add a third cog, then it turns in the same direction as the first cog.

first cog

If you turn the first cog, how many of the other cogs in this photograph will turn?

The cogs inside gears are not always right next to each other. Cogs can be joined together by belts or chains.

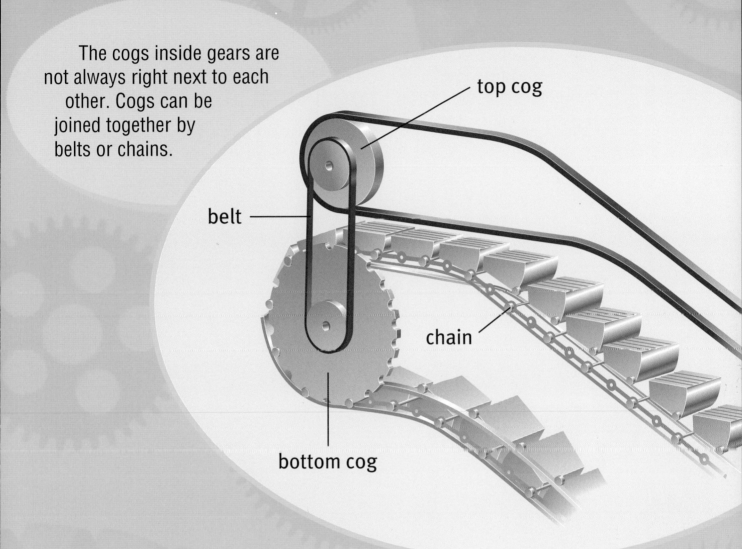

top cog

belt

chain

bottom cog

An escalator is a machine that you use instead of stairs. It uses gears. A **motor** turns the top cog. A belt joins the teeth of the top cog to the teeth in the bottom cog. This means that one motor can turn two cogs. When cogs are joined with a belt or chain, they turn in the same direction.

How Do We Use Gears?

We can use gears to change the speed of something that turns. To do this, we need different sized **cogs** working together.

Cogs work together to control the speed of this toy car.

Activity

Fast to slow . . .
1. Find one plastic cog with 24 teeth and one smaller cog with 12 teeth.
2. Join the cogs by locking the teeth.
3. Turn the small cog around for one full circle. The small cog has moved 12 teeth, and so has the large cog. The large cog is moving more slowly, so it has only moved half a circle.

Slow to fast . . .
1. Now, turn the large cog in one circle. What happens?

A windmill is a machine that uses gears to **grind** up grain into flour. The wind blows the sails around. This makes a large cog turn. This cog is joined to a smaller cog. The small cog is joined to stones called millstones. The millstones grind the grain. They turn quickly because they are joined to the small cog.

This windmill uses gears to help it grind up grain.

sails

Bicycle Gears

On a bicycle, gears of different sizes are fixed together. The gear **cog** by the pedal and the gear cogs of the back wheel are linked together by a chain. This fits over the teeth of the cogs. The chain always stays around the pedal gear cog, but it can move between the different sized back gear cogs.

When you change gear, the chain lifts off one gear cog and onto another.

The cog joined to the pedals drives all the cogs. You make this gear turn by pushing the pedals with your feet.

20

When you start moving on a bicycle or try to ride up a hill, the wheels of the bicycle need a large **force** to turn them. You need the pedals to move the largest gear cog at the back. This means that the bicycle wheels will turn at a low speed, but with a large force. You will therefore need less force to push on the pedals.

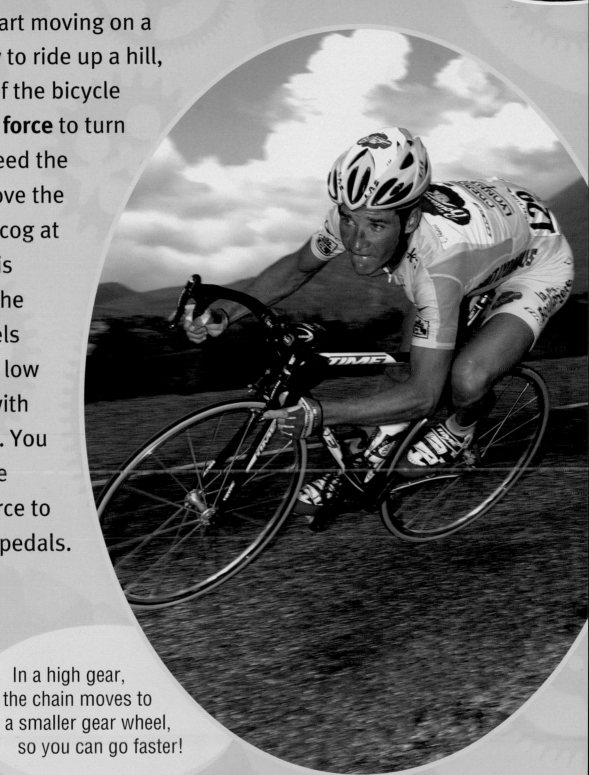

In a high gear, the chain moves to a smaller gear wheel, so you can go faster!

Groovy Gears

Special gears called **worm gears** can be used to change the direction and speed of a turn. A worm gear has a **rod** with a screw shape on it. It also has a **cog** with teeth that fit into the spaces in the screw.

Worm gears are useful because they can slow down movement. When you turn the cog quickly, the rod with the screw moves much more slowly.

When you turn the cog, the teeth push against the spaces in the screw and make it turn slowly.

screw

cog

Another type of gear is called a **rack and pinion.** This gear can turn turning movement into back and forth movement.

A rack and pinion is made up of a cog and a straight piece of metal with teeth in it. When the cog turns, the teeth push against the teeth of the piece of metal. It moves forward or backward.

Some car windows use a rack and pinion gear. When the handle turns around, the window moves up and down.

Gears in the House and Garden

A lawn sprinkler is a machine that uses lots of gears. The water flows into the sprinkler and turns a wheel called a turbine. The water then pushes out through holes in the top of the sprinkler.

The turbine spins very fast, so there are some **worm gears** inside that slow down the movement. The slow movement then drives a **crank.** The crank changes the turning movement into a side-to-side movement, so that the water reaches a large part of your garden.

Lots of **simple machines** work together inside a lawn sprinkler.

Some beaters use gears. A handle is joined to a large **cog.** The large cog is connected with teeth to two smaller cogs. When the large cog turns, it makes the small cogs turn quickly.

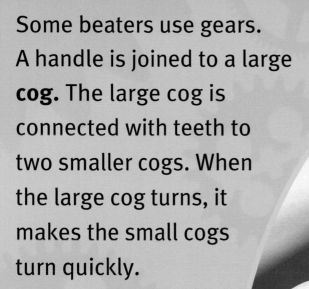

Activity

1. Ask an adult if he or she has an beater like the one in this picture.
2. Turn the handle so that you make just one whole circle with the large cog. As you do this, see if you can count how many times the ends of the beater turn around.

Cars

All cars have gears to make the car wheels turn at different speeds. A car also needs a gear **cog** that will make the wheels turn. This allows the car to turn corners. The drive shaft is a **rod** that joins the gearbox to the wheels of the car. In a low gear, the car wheels turn slowly. In a high gear, they turn very fast.

Can you see how many different cogs there are inside this gearbox?

There are many other gears inside a car. In some cars, the speedometer measures how fast the car is going. It also counts how many miles or kilometers the car has traveled since it was made.

Gears can be used to show how far a car has traveled.

The dials that show how far the car has traveled are connected to the wheels of the car. As the car moves, the car wheels turn. As the car wheels turn, the dials turn. The dials need to turn much more slowly than the car wheels, and so a **worm gear** is used to slow them down.

The Clockwork Radio

The clockwork radio was **invented** in 1994. It uses lots of **simple machines** inside it.

1. Handle: You turn the handle to wind up the metal spring (see #2). When you stop winding, the spring wants to return to the shape it was before.

2. Spring: The spring unwinds slowly and turns the **axle** in the middle of the spring.

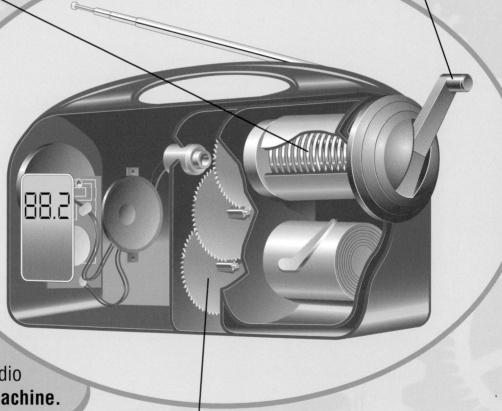

The clockwork radio is a **compound machine**.

3. Gears: The gears are used to turn the slow movement into fast movement that can make electricity. As the fast gear **cog** turns, it makes electricity that allows the radio to work.

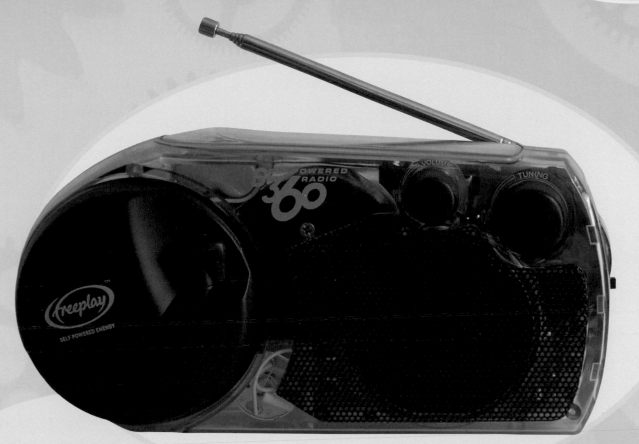

A clockwork radio doesn't need electricity to make it work. You give it power by winding it up.

The clockwork radio is very important for people in places where there is no electricity supply. A radio helps people learn what is happening in the world and gives them important information when there is an emergency.

All sorts of machines use pulleys and gears to do lots of different things. Take a look around your house and see how many you can find!

Find Out for Yourself

You can find out about pulleys and gears by talking to your teacher or parents. Think about the **simple machines** you use every day. How do you think they work? Your local library will have books and information about this. You will find the answers to many of your questions in this book, but you can also use other books and the Internet.

Books to read

Douglas, Lloyd G. *What Is a Pulley?* Danbury, Conn.: Scholastic Library Publishing, 2003.

Oxlade, Chris. *Very Useful Machines: Pulleys*. Chicago, Ill.: Heinemann Library, 2003.

Using the Internet

Explore the Internet to find out more about pulleys and gears. Try using a search engine such as www.yahooligans.com or www.internet4kids.com, and type in keywords such as "pulley," "gear," and **"worm gear."**

Glossary

axle thin bar (rod) that goes through the center of a wheel or group of wheels

cog wheel with teeth around the edge

combined pulley pulley made up of a fixed pulley and a movable pulley working together

compound machine machine that uses two or more simple machines

crank part of a machine that changes turning movement into side-to-side movement

effort force push or pull that you put into a pulley or gear to move or lift something

engine machine that can make things move

fixed pulley pulley that changes the direction of the pull you put into it

force push or pull used to move or lift something

grind smash up into little pieces

invent discover or make something for the first time

mechanical advantage when a machine is used to turn the small force (amount of push or pull) you provide into a larger force

motor machine that can make things move. Motors usually work using electricity.

movable pulley pulley that makes the pull you put into it bigger. It helps you lift heavy objects.

rack and pinion gear that changes turning movement into back and forth movement

rod thin bar, usually made of metal or wood

simple machine something that can change the effort force (push or pull you provide) needed to move something or change the direction it moves

worm gear screw and cog working together

Index

JUV
621.833
Sadler   Sadler, Wendy

        **Using pulleys and
        gears**

DUE DATE
